What are....?

VOLCANOES

Claire Llewellyn

For more information about Heinemann Library books, or to order, please telephone +44 (0)1865 888066, or send a fax to +44 (0)1865 314091. You can visit our web site at www.heinemann.co.uk

First published in Great Britain by Heinemann Library,
Halley Court, Jordan Hill, Oxford OX2 8EJ
a division of Reed Educational and Professional Publishing Ltd.
Heinemann is a registered trademark of Reed Educational & Professional Publishing Ltd.

OXFORD MELBOURNE AUCKLAND
JOHANNESBURG BLANTYRE GABORONE
IBADAN PORTSMOUTH (NH) USA CHICAGO

Designed by David Oakley
Illustrations by Hardlines (p.7) and Jo Brooker
Printed in China

05
10 9 8 7 6 5 4 3
ISBN 978 0 431 02382 3
ISBN 0 431 02382 4

British Library Cataloguing in Publication Data
This book is also available in a hardback library edition (ISBN 0 431 02376 X)

Llewellyn, Claire
  What are volcanoes?
  1. Volcanoes – Juvenile literature
  1. Title II. Volcanoes
  551.2'1

Acknowledgements
The Publishers would like to thank the following for permission to reproduce photographs:
Colorific!: Baron Sakiya p.12; FLPA: AA Riley p.5, A Nardi/Panda Photo p.26, USGS p.6, USDA Forest Service p.13, S Jonasson p.14, R Holcomb p.18, Jurgen & Christine Sohns p.20; NASA: Johnson Space Centre p.22, p.24; Oxford Scientific Films: Survival Anglia/Joan Root p.4, Frank Huber p.10, David B Fleetham p.15; Robert Harding Picture Library: Adina Tovy p.8, AC Waltham p.9, Kim Hart p.19, Tony Waltham p.21; Science Photo Library: NASA p.11; Still Pictures: Reinhard Janke p.16, John Cancalosi p.17; Trip: p.29, P Nicholas p.28.

Cover photograph reproduced with permission of Robert Harding Picture Library.

Every effort has been made to contact copyright holders of any material reproduced in this book. Any omissions will be rectified in subsequent printings if notice is given to the Publisher.

Contents

Some words are shown in bold, **like this**.
You can find out what they mean by looking
in the Glossary.

What is a volcano?

Inside a volcano is a hole which goes down into the middle of the Earth. When it **erupts**, it shoots out red-hot liquid rock and ash from deep inside the Earth.

A stream of liquid rock pours out of a volcano.

When the hot rock comes out of the volcano it is called **lava**. The lava then cools and hardens. This slowly builds the volcano up into a mountain. It may be years before the volcano erupts again.

The sides of this volcano are made of solid lava.

What starts a volcano?

The Earth is made of rock. On the surface of the Earth, the rock is cool and hard. Underneath the rock is hot and liquid. It tries to squeeze out of any holes in the Earth's surface.

This hot rock comes from inside the Earth.

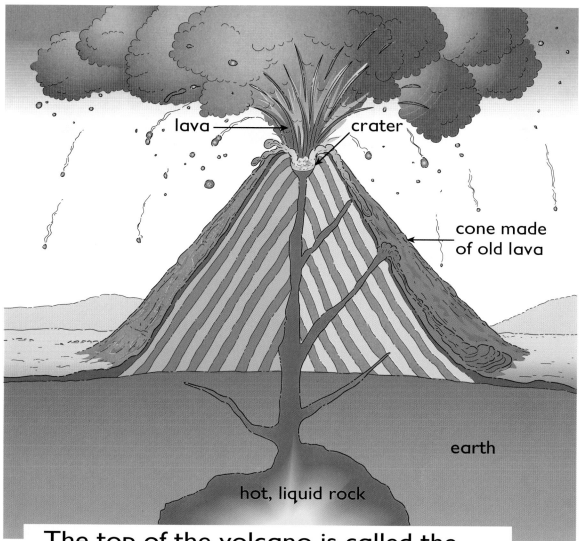

lava crater

cone made of old lava

earth

hot, liquid rock

The top of the volcano is called the **crater**. The sides are called the **cone**.

A volcano is like a chimney with a large opening at the top. The hot, liquid rock is pushed up the chimney. It bursts out of the top. When it **erupts** the rock is called **lava**.

Building a volcano

Mount Fuji in Japan has very steep sides.

Sometimes, the **lava** is so thick that it runs downhill very slowly. As it hardens, it builds a mountain with very steep sides.

Mauna Loa on the island of
Hawaii has gently sloping sides.

Sometimes, the lava is thin and runs
downhill very fast. As it hardens, it builds
a wider mountain with gentler slopes.

Volcano s in the s a

Many volcanoes rise up from the sea-bed. Each time they **erupt**, they grow a little higher until their peaks make islands in the sea.

This island is in Alaska. It is the top of an undersea volcano.

Sometimes a line of undersea volcanoes grow above the surface of the water. Their peaks make a long line of islands in the sea.

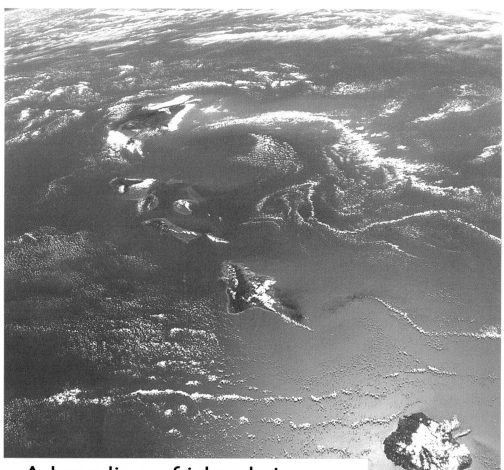

A long line of islands is called an island arc.

Different eruptions

Volcanoes that **erupt** regularly are called **active** volcanoes. Some erupt gently. The **lava** seeps out quietly and the gas comes out in puffs.

This volcano is Mauna Loa in Hawaii. It is erupting quietly.

Mount St Helens erupted violently in 1980.

Other volcanoes erupt like a bomb going off. Sometimes, a part of the mountain may be destroyed. Part of the **cone** of Mount St Helens in America was blown away.

The power of volcanoes

Volcanoes have a sudden and deadly power. The hot **lava** can destroy towns and kill people. The ash from the volcano can crush houses and plants.

Ash from this volcano has buried these houses.

This stream of lava is flowing over a road.
Nothing can stop it.

When lava pours out of a volcano, it
burns everything in its path. It flattens
trees and crops, and covers the land.

Using volcanoes

These fields lie at the very foot of a volcano in Spain.

Volcanoes can be useful. The ash and **lava** make the ground very good for farming. Crops grow well in the earth on the slopes.

The rocks near volcanoes are very hot. Power stations use them to heat water. This helps them to make electricity for factories and homes.

The steam made from the water helps to drive machines.

Studying volcanoes

Scientists who study volcanoes are called **vulcanologists**. They measure volcanoes and check for movements in the ground.

This vulcanologist is measuring how fast the **lava** is moving.

Scientists work in this **observatory** on a volcano. It is in Hawaii.

Scientists learn lots of things from studying volcanoes. They use the results to try to predict when a volcano will next **erupt**. This could save many people's lives.

Old volcanoes

Volcanoes that have not **erupted** for many years are called **dormant** volcanoes. We sometimes say they are sleeping.

Mount Kilimanjaro in Kenya, Africa, is a dormant volcano.

The sides of this volcano have been worn away by wind and rain.

Volcanoes that will never erupt again are called **extinct** volcanoes. Their **cones** are slowly worn down by the weather.

Volcano map 1

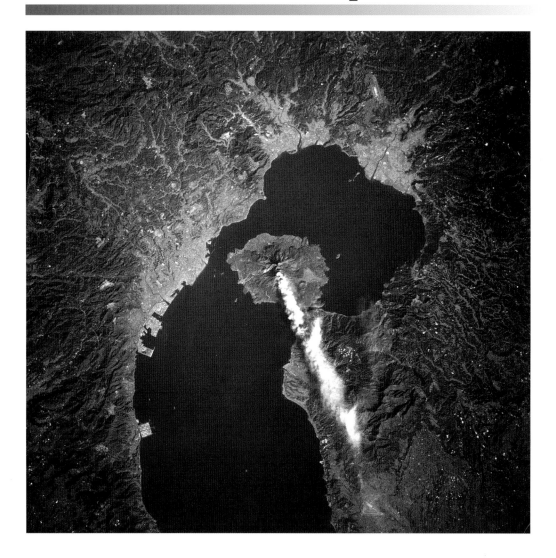

This is a photo of a volcano. It was taken by a **satellite** high above the earth. The volcano is an island just off the coast. It is surrounded by sea.

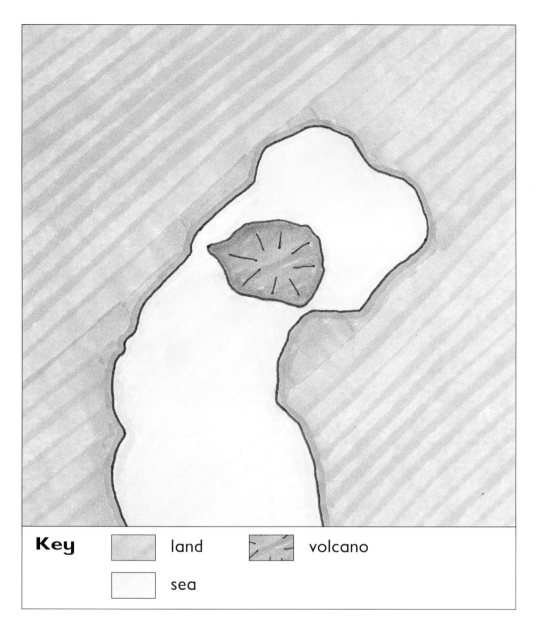

Maps are pictures of the land. This map shows us the same place as the photo. The key tells us what each colour means. The blue colour shows the sea. The brown colour shows the land.

Volcano map 2

This photo shows a smaller part of the land but you can see it more clearly. The volcano looks bigger. You can see a cloud of ash coming out of it. You can see a city on the coast.

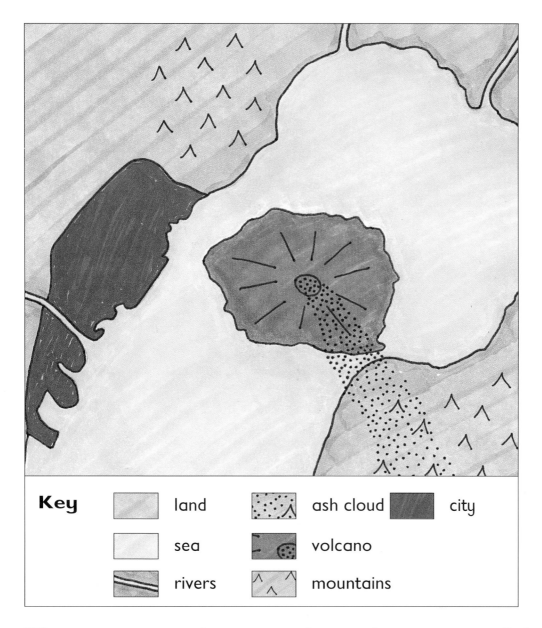

Key

land	ash cloud	city
sea	volcano	
rivers	mountains	

The points on this map show that some of the land is very high above the sea. The red colour shows the buildings in the city. The black dots show ash coming out of the volcano.

Volcano map 3

This photo shows another volcano. It was taken from an aeroplane. It does not show the whole volcano, but you can see inside the **crater** very clearly.

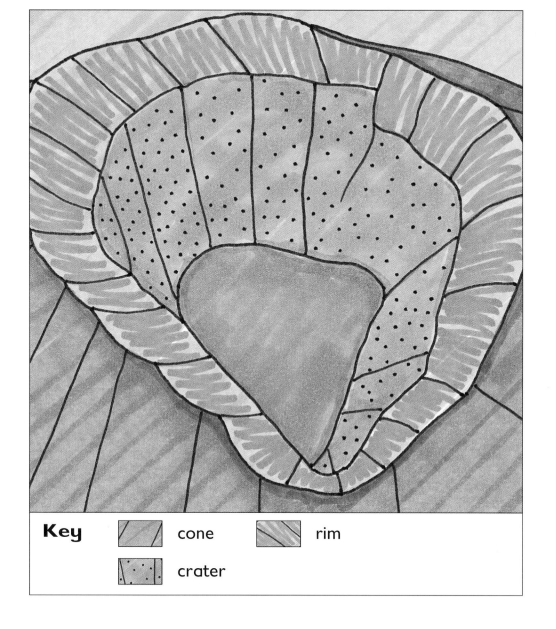

Key cone rim crater

The sides of the volcano are very steep. At the rim of the crater the land sinks down steeply to the middle. The map shows the steep slopes of the **cone** with thin black lines.

Amazing volcano facts

About 2000 years ago Mount Vesuvius in Italy suddenly **erupted**. It buried the Roman town of Pompeii. You can now visit the ruins of the town.

Mauna Kea, an island in Hawaii, is the top of an undersea volcano. It measures 10,205 metres from the sea-bed to the peak – that makes it taller than Mount Everest!

Glossary

active a volcano that is able to erupt

cone the sides of a volcano

crater the large round opening at the top of a volcano

dormant a volcano that has not erupted for many years

erupt to suddenly shoot out lava and ash

extinct a volcano that will never erupt again

lava the hot, liquid rock that shoots out of a volcano from inside the Earth

observatory a special building where people like scientists can watch a volcano and make measurements

satellite a special machine in space which goes round the Earth and can take photographs

vulcanologist a person who studies volcanoes

More books to read

Daniel Rogers.
Geography Starts Here! Volcano.
Wayland, 1998

Claire Llewellyn.
Why do we have... Rocks and Mountains?
Heinemann, 1997

Andy Owen and Miranda Ashwell.
What Are... Mountains?
Heinemann, 1998

Daphne Butler.
What happens when Volcanoes Erupt?
Simon and Schuster, 1993

Index